Thank you very much for reading this book.

Title: AI Revolution in Law-Opportunities and Challenges
Subtitle: From Legal Research to Predictive Analytics and Beyond

Series: Rise of Cognitive Computing: AI Evolution from Origins to Adoption
Author: Herman Strange

Table of Contents

Introduction 6

What is AI, and How Does it Apply to the Legal Industry? 6

The Impact of AI on the Legal Industry 9

Overview of the Book 12

Chapter 1: AI and Legal Research 15

AI-assisted Legal Research 15

Natural Language Processing and Machine Learning for Legal Research 18

Impact of AI on the Legal Research Industry 21

Potential Challenges and Limitations of AI in Legal Research 24

Chapter 2: AI and Contract Review 26

AI-assisted Contract Review 26

Use Cases for AI in Contract Review 29

Impact of AI on Contract Review Industry 31

Potential Challenges and Limitations of AI in Contract Review 33

Chapter 3: AI and Predictive Analytics in Law 35

Overview of Predictive Analytics and Machine Learning Algorithms for Legal Predictions 35

Benefits of Predictive Analytics for the Legal Industry .. 37

Legal Use Cases for Predictive Analytics and Machine Learning 39

Potential Ethical Implications of Predictive Analytics in Law 42

Chapter 4: AI and Intellectual Property Law **45**

AI Applications in Intellectual Property Law 45

AI-generated Inventions and Patent Law 50

Legal Issues Surrounding AI-generated Content 53

Challenges of Regulating AI in Intellectual Property Law 56

Chapter 5: AI and E-Discovery **60**

AI-assisted E-Discovery 60

Use Cases for AI in E-Discovery 62

Impact of AI on E-Discovery Industry 64

Potential Challenges and Limitations of AI in E-Discovery 67

Chapter 6: AI and Legal Writing **69**

AI-assisted Legal Writing 69

Natural Language Generation and Machine Learning for Legal Writing 72

Impact of AI on Legal Writing Industry 74

Potential Challenges and Limitations of AI in Legal Writing 77

Chapter 7: AI and the Future of the Legal Industry 79

The Potential Future of AI in Law 79

Impact of AI on the Legal Profession and Legal Education 82

Ethical Implications of AI in Law 85

Opportunities and Challenges for the Legal Industry in the Age of AI 88

Conclusion **93**

The Potential Future of AI in Law and Its Impact on Society 93

The Importance of Continued Research and Development in AI for Law 96

The Need for Ethical and Responsible AI Development and Use in the Legal Industry 98

Key Formulas and Glossary **101**

Potential References **103**

Introduction
What is AI, and How Does it Apply to the Legal Industry?

Artificial Intelligence (AI) has become a ubiquitous term in today's technology-driven world. It refers to a wide range of technologies that enable machines to perform tasks that typically require human-like intelligence. These tasks can include understanding natural language, recognizing patterns, making decisions, and more.

In the legal industry, AI has the potential to revolutionize the way lawyers work by improving efficiency, accuracy, and speed. AI can assist lawyers in a wide range of tasks, from legal research and document review to contract analysis and predicting case outcomes. In this section, we will explore the basics of AI and its applications in the legal industry.

What is AI?

AI is a broad field that encompasses many different technologies, including machine learning, natural language processing, and computer vision, to name a few. At its core, AI aims to enable machines to perform tasks that typically require human-like intelligence, such as reasoning, learning, problem-solving, and decision-making.

Machine learning is a subset of AI that involves training machines to learn from data, without being explicitly programmed. Natural language processing, on the other hand, involves enabling machines to understand and process human language. Computer vision involves enabling machines to interpret and analyze visual data.

AI and the Legal Industry

In recent years, the legal industry has seen an increasing use of AI in a wide range of applications. AI can assist lawyers in tasks such as legal research, contract analysis, document review, and predicting case outcomes. AI-powered tools can help lawyers to work more efficiently, accurately, and quickly, ultimately improving the quality of legal services provided to clients.

AI has the potential to transform the legal industry by enabling lawyers to focus on higher-level tasks such as strategy and counseling, while automating routine and repetitive tasks. Additionally, AI can help to identify patterns and insights that may not be immediately apparent to humans, ultimately improving decision-making and outcomes.

In this section, we will explore the different applications of AI in the legal industry, including its potential benefits and challenges. We will also examine the role of lawyers in developing and implementing AI systems and discuss some of the ethical considerations surrounding the use of AI in the legal industry.

Conclusion

AI is a powerful technology that has the potential to transform the legal industry by improving efficiency, accuracy, and speed. It can assist lawyers in tasks ranging from legal research and document review to contract analysis and predicting case outcomes. However, as with any new technology, there are potential challenges and ethical considerations that need to be addressed. In the following chapters, we will explore these issues in more detail and examine the various applications of AI in the legal industry.

Artificial Intelligence has been a game-changer in many industries, and the legal industry is no exception. The impact of AI on the legal industry has been significant, and it has transformed the way legal professionals work. In this section, we will explore the impact of AI on the legal industry and how it has revolutionized the way lawyers and law firms operate.

1. Improved Efficiency and Productivity AI has improved the efficiency and productivity of legal professionals by automating repetitive tasks and streamlining workflows. For example, AI-powered legal research tools can quickly analyze vast amounts of data, helping lawyers save time and effort. Similarly, AI-enabled contract review software can automatically identify key clauses, reducing the time and effort required for manual review.

2. Enhanced Accuracy and Consistency AI has also improved the accuracy and consistency of legal work. By reducing the chances of human error, AI-powered tools have increased the reliability of legal documents and processes. For example, AI-powered contract review software can identify inconsistencies and errors in legal contracts,

reducing the risk of legal disputes and ensuring compliance with legal requirements.

3. Cost Savings AI has also led to significant cost savings in the legal industry. By automating repetitive tasks and reducing the need for manual labor, AI-powered tools have reduced the overall cost of legal services. For example, AI-powered legal research tools can reduce the time required for legal research, leading to lower billing hours and cost savings for clients.

4. Increased Access to Legal Services AI has also increased access to legal services, particularly for low-income individuals who may not be able to afford traditional legal services. AI-powered tools, such as chatbots and virtual assistants, can provide legal information and support at a lower cost, making legal services more accessible to a wider audience.

5. New Legal Issues and Ethical Considerations AI has also brought new legal issues and ethical considerations to the forefront. For example, AI-generated content and AI-powered decision-making raise questions about the responsibility and accountability of legal professionals. As AI becomes more prevalent in the legal industry, it is important to address these issues and ensure that legal professionals adhere to ethical and legal standards.

In conclusion, AI has had a significant impact on the legal industry, improving efficiency, accuracy, and cost-effectiveness, while also raising new legal issues and ethical considerations. As AI continues to evolve, it is important for legal professionals to adapt to these changes and embrace the opportunities that AI presents.

Overview of the Book

In this section, we will provide an overview of the contents of this book, chapter by chapter. We will summarize the key themes, topics, and issues that will be explored in each chapter, and explain how they fit into the broader narrative of the book.

Chapter 1: The Basics of AI for Lawyers In this chapter, we will introduce the basic concepts of artificial intelligence and its applications in the legal industry. We will discuss the benefits and challenges of AI adoption in law firms, and the role of lawyers in developing and implementing AI systems.

Chapter 2: AI and Legal Research This chapter will explore the use of AI in legal research, focusing on natural language processing and machine learning for legal research. We will discuss the benefits of AI-assisted legal research and the potential challenges and limitations of AI in legal research.

Chapter 3: AI and Contract Review In this chapter, we will examine the use of AI in contract review, including use cases for AI in contract review, the impact of AI on the contract review industry, and potential challenges and limitations of AI in contract review.

Chapter 4: AI and Predictive Analytics in the Legal Industry In this chapter, we will provide an overview of predictive analytics and machine learning algorithms for legal predictions. We will discuss the benefits of predictive analytics for the legal industry, legal use cases for predictive analytics and machine learning, and potential ethical implications of predictive analytics in law.

Chapter 5: AI and Intellectual Property Law This chapter will examine the application of AI in intellectual property law, including AI-generated inventions and patent law, legal issues surrounding AI-generated content, and the challenges of regulating AI in intellectual property law.

Chapter 6: AI and the Future of the Legal Industry In this chapter, we will explore the potential future of AI in the legal industry, including its impact on the legal profession and legal education, the ethical implications of AI in law, and potential challenges and opportunities for the legal industry in the age of AI.

Chapter 7: AI and Ethics in the Legal Industry This chapter will examine the ethical considerations surrounding the use of AI in the legal industry, including issues related to bias, privacy, and accountability. We will discuss the need for ethical and responsible AI development and use in the legal industry.

Conclusion In the conclusion, we will summarize the key themes and takeaways from the book. We will discuss the potential future of AI in law and its impact on society, the need for continued research and development in AI for law, and the importance of ethical and responsible AI development and use in the legal industry. Finally, we will provide recommendations for further reading and research.

Chapter 1: AI and Legal Research
AI-assisted Legal Research

Legal research is an essential aspect of legal practice. Lawyers, paralegals, and other legal professionals often spend countless hours searching for relevant cases, statutes, and regulations that pertain to their clients' legal issues. Artificial intelligence (AI) has the potential to revolutionize legal research by automating many of the tedious and time-consuming aspects of the process.

AI can assist legal research in several ways. One of the most promising approaches is through natural language processing (NLP), which allows computers to understand and interpret human language. By applying NLP techniques to legal documents and databases, AI systems can identify and extract relevant information more quickly and accurately than humans.

AI can also assist legal research by automating document review and analysis. In many cases, lawyers must review vast amounts of documents, such as contracts, emails, and other correspondence, to identify relevant information. AI-powered document review systems can automate this process, significantly reducing the time and effort required to review large volumes of documents.

Another way that AI can assist legal research is through predictive analytics. Predictive analytics involves using machine learning algorithms to identify patterns and make predictions based on historical data. In the legal context, predictive analytics can help lawyers and other legal professionals anticipate legal outcomes and identify potential risks or opportunities.

One of the most significant benefits of AI-assisted legal research is its potential to reduce errors and increase accuracy. Legal research is a highly complex and specialized task, requiring a deep understanding of legal concepts, terminology, and procedures. Even the most skilled legal professionals are susceptible to mistakes or oversights. AI systems can analyze vast amounts of data quickly and accurately, reducing the likelihood of errors or omissions.

Despite its many potential benefits, AI-assisted legal research also raises significant ethical and practical concerns. For example, some have raised concerns about the accuracy and reliability of AI systems, particularly with respect to issues such as bias and discrimination. Others have raised concerns about the impact of AI on employment in the legal industry and the potential for AI to replace human legal professionals.

In conclusion, AI-assisted legal research has the potential to revolutionize the legal industry by automating many of the tedious and time-consuming aspects of legal research. By using NLP, document review, and predictive analytics, AI systems can help legal professionals identify and extract relevant information more quickly and accurately than humans. However, these systems also raise significant ethical and practical concerns that must be addressed to ensure that AI is used responsibly and effectively in the legal industry.

Natural Language Processing and Machine Learning for Legal Research

Natural language processing (NLP) and machine learning (ML) are two key technologies that have contributed to the development of AI-assisted legal research. NLP is a subfield of computer science and artificial intelligence concerned with the interaction between computers and human (natural) languages. It focuses on the ability of computers to understand, interpret, and generate human language. On the other hand, machine learning is a type of artificial intelligence that enables computers to learn and improve from experience without being explicitly programmed.

NLP and ML have transformed the way legal research is conducted by providing advanced tools for text analysis, information retrieval, and knowledge discovery. NLP-based techniques can help lawyers and legal professionals to search, analyze, and extract relevant information from large volumes of unstructured legal texts such as case law, statutes, regulations, and legal contracts. By automating the process of legal research, NLP and ML technologies can save time, reduce costs, and improve the quality of legal services.

One of the most promising applications of NLP in legal research is legal text classification. Legal text classification involves the categorization of legal texts into predefined categories or topics. This can be achieved by training machine learning models on annotated legal datasets. These models can then be used to automatically classify new legal texts into relevant categories or topics. Legal text classification can help lawyers and legal professionals to quickly find relevant legal information and improve the accuracy of legal research.

Another important application of NLP in legal research is named entity recognition (NER). NER involves the identification and extraction of named entities such as persons, organizations, and locations from legal texts. This can be useful for various legal applications such as contract review, due diligence, and litigation support. NER can also be used to identify relationships between named entities, which can help in identifying patterns and trends in legal data.

In addition to NLP, machine learning algorithms can be used for predictive legal analytics, which involves the analysis of legal data to identify patterns and make predictions about legal outcomes. Predictive legal analytics can help lawyers and legal professionals to make better decisions and provide more accurate legal advice to clients. For example, machine learning algorithms can be used to predict the likelihood of a legal case being successful based on past case outcomes and other relevant legal data.

Overall, NLP and ML technologies have significant potential for improving the efficiency and effectiveness of legal research. However, there are also challenges and limitations associated with their use. These include issues related to data quality, bias, and interpretability. Therefore, it is important for legal professionals to be aware of these issues and adopt responsible and ethical practices when using AI-assisted legal research tools.

Impact of AI on the Legal Research Industry

The legal research industry has undergone a significant transformation in recent years with the advent of artificial intelligence (AI) technology. The impact of AI on the legal research industry has been profound, and it has revolutionized the way legal professionals conduct research.

AI technology has transformed the legal research industry in several ways. One of the primary benefits of AI technology is that it has enabled legal professionals to conduct research more quickly and accurately. AI algorithms are capable of processing vast amounts of data in a short period, which enables legal professionals to quickly access and analyze relevant information. Additionally, AI algorithms are capable of analyzing large data sets to identify patterns and trends, which can be used to inform legal research.

Another way in which AI has impacted the legal research industry is by enabling legal professionals to conduct research more efficiently. With AI algorithms, legal professionals can automate repetitive tasks such as document review and analysis, which frees up their time to focus on more complex legal issues. This has helped to increase productivity and reduce the time and cost associated with legal research.

AI technology has also democratized legal research by making it more accessible to a broader range of people. Traditionally, legal research has been the domain of legal professionals who have access to expensive legal databases and resources. However, AI technology has enabled legal research to be conducted by a wider range of people, including law students, researchers, and members of the public.

Despite the numerous benefits of AI technology for legal research, there are also potential downsides that need to be considered. One of the primary concerns is the accuracy of AI algorithms. While AI algorithms can process vast amounts of data quickly, there is a risk that they may produce inaccurate results if the data input is flawed or biased. Additionally, there is a risk that AI algorithms may perpetuate existing biases in the legal system if they are trained on biased data sets.

Another concern is the potential impact of AI technology on employment in the legal research industry. While AI technology has the potential to increase productivity and efficiency, it may also lead to job losses as certain tasks become automated. This could have significant implications for legal professionals who rely on legal research as a source of employment.

In conclusion, the impact of AI on the legal research industry has been significant, and it has revolutionized the way legal professionals conduct research. AI technology has enabled legal professionals to conduct research more quickly, accurately, and efficiently, which has increased productivity and reduced the time and cost associated with legal research. However, there are also potential downsides that need to be considered, including the accuracy of AI algorithms, the potential perpetuation of biases, and the impact on employment in the legal research industry.

Potential Challenges and Limitations of AI in Legal Research

AI has the potential to revolutionize the legal research industry, but it also comes with its own set of challenges and limitations. In this section, we will discuss some of the potential drawbacks of AI-assisted legal research.

1. Lack of Transparency One of the most significant concerns about AI in legal research is the lack of transparency in how algorithms work. Since AI is programmed to learn from data, it may be difficult to understand how it came up with a particular conclusion. Lawyers and researchers may find it difficult to challenge the results of AI algorithms without a clear understanding of how they arrived at their conclusions.

2. Limited Availability of Data AI algorithms require vast amounts of data to be trained effectively. However, legal research data is not always widely available, and even when it is, it may be in different formats, making it difficult for AI systems to process.

3. Cost AI technology can be expensive, particularly for smaller law firms and individual researchers. The cost of implementing AI in legal research may outweigh the benefits, particularly for those with limited budgets.

4. Potential for Bias AI algorithms may also be susceptible to bias, particularly if they are trained on biased data. This could lead to unintended discriminatory outcomes, which would be particularly problematic in legal settings where fairness is crucial.

5. Limitations of AI Technology AI technology is not perfect and has its own limitations. For example, AI may not be able to understand the context of legal cases as well as human lawyers. AI algorithms may also be limited in their ability to interpret complex legal texts or statutes.

6. Ethical Concerns There are also ethical concerns surrounding the use of AI in legal research, particularly when it comes to privacy and data protection. AI systems may also raise ethical concerns about the appropriate use of technology in legal decision-making processes.

In conclusion, while AI has the potential to revolutionize legal research, it is not without its challenges and limitations. It is essential to recognize and address these potential drawbacks to ensure that the benefits of AI can be realized while minimizing any negative impacts.

Chapter 2: AI and Contract Review

AI-assisted Contract Review

Contract review is a critical task in the legal industry, as it involves the careful analysis of legal documents to identify potential issues and ensure compliance with relevant laws and regulations. With the help of AI technology, contract review can be made more efficient and accurate. AI-assisted contract review involves the use of machine learning algorithms and natural language processing to analyze contracts and identify relevant clauses, provisions, and obligations.

The use of AI in contract review can help legal professionals to streamline their work and improve the accuracy of their analyses. AI can be trained to identify common clauses and provisions in contracts, which can help legal professionals to quickly identify potential issues and areas of concern. AI can also be used to identify inconsistencies or conflicts within contracts, which can help to reduce the risk of legal disputes arising in the future.

One of the main benefits of AI-assisted contract review is its ability to process large volumes of data quickly and accurately. AI algorithms can analyze thousands of contracts in a matter of minutes, which would be impossible for a human legal professional to do in the same amount of time. This can be especially useful in cases where legal teams need to review large volumes of contracts, such as in mergers and acquisitions or in regulatory compliance.

AI-assisted contract review can also help legal professionals to reduce their workload and focus on more complex legal tasks. By automating routine contract review tasks, legal professionals can devote more time and attention to analyzing legal issues and developing effective legal strategies.

However, there are also potential challenges and limitations associated with the use of AI in contract review. One challenge is the need for accurate data input. The accuracy of AI algorithms relies on the quality of the data that is fed into them. Inaccurate or incomplete data can lead to inaccurate results and unreliable analyses.

Another challenge is the need for effective training and development of AI algorithms. AI algorithms require extensive training and development to ensure that they can accurately identify relevant clauses and provisions in contracts. Legal professionals need to be involved in the training and development process to ensure that AI algorithms are being trained to accurately analyze legal language and identify potential legal issues.

In addition, there are also concerns about the potential biases that can be introduced into AI algorithms. AI algorithms are only as objective as the data that is fed into them, and there is a risk that biases can be introduced into the algorithms if the data used to train them is not representative of the wider population.

Overall, AI-assisted contract review has the potential to revolutionize the legal industry by making contract review more efficient and accurate. However, it is important for legal professionals to be aware of the potential challenges and limitations associated with the use of AI in contract review and to take steps to address these issues to ensure that AI is being used effectively and responsibly.

Use Cases for AI in Contract Review

Artificial intelligence (AI) has significant potential to revolutionize the process of contract review. Legal professionals can leverage AI technologies to analyze, extract, and classify relevant data from contracts, speeding up the review process and reducing errors. Here are some use cases for AI in contract review:

1. Due Diligence Review: AI can be used to conduct a comprehensive review of all contracts related to a specific company, industry, or transaction. The AI-powered system can extract information from all contracts, identify relevant clauses and provisions, and flag any anomalies or discrepancies.

2. Clause Extraction and Standardization: AI can be used to identify and extract specific clauses from contracts, such as indemnification clauses, confidentiality provisions, and termination clauses. These clauses can then be standardized to ensure consistency and efficiency in contract management.

3. Risk Assessment: AI can help legal professionals identify and assess the risk associated with specific contracts. By analyzing the language used in contracts and comparing it to similar contracts, AI can identify potential issues, such as conflicts of interest or unclear terms.

4. Contract Review for Mergers and Acquisitions: AI can help legal professionals review contracts related to mergers and acquisitions, a process that can be time-consuming and labor-intensive. AI can identify any clauses that may pose a risk to the transaction and help legal professionals make informed decisions.

5. Compliance Review: AI can be used to ensure that contracts comply with regulatory requirements, such as GDPR or HIPAA. The AI system can flag any clauses or provisions that may violate these regulations, helping legal professionals to ensure compliance.

6. Contract Analytics: AI can be used to analyze large sets of contracts, providing insights into trends, patterns, and anomalies. By analyzing historical data, legal professionals can make better decisions, identify areas for improvement, and reduce risks.

While these use cases demonstrate the potential benefits of AI in contract review, it is important to note that AI is not a silver bullet. There are limitations and potential challenges associated with AI in contract review, which must be addressed to ensure successful implementation.

Impact of AI on Contract Review Industry

AI has the potential to revolutionize the way contracts are reviewed and managed. Contract review is a time-consuming and labor-intensive task that requires a high level of attention to detail. AI technologies can help streamline this process and reduce the risk of errors.

One of the primary benefits of using AI for contract review is increased efficiency. AI can quickly and accurately analyze large volumes of contracts and extract relevant information, such as key terms, clauses, and obligations. This can save legal professionals a significant amount of time and effort, freeing them up to focus on higher-level tasks.

Another benefit of AI in contract review is increased accuracy. AI algorithms can analyze contracts with a level of precision and consistency that is difficult to achieve manually. This can help identify potential risks and issues, such as non-compliance with regulations or conflicting clauses, that may have otherwise gone unnoticed.

AI can also provide insights into contract data that can help inform business decisions. By analyzing large volumes of contract data, AI can identify trends, patterns, and anomalies that can help organizations better understand their contractual relationships and improve their overall contract management strategies.

In addition to these benefits, AI can also help mitigate the risk of human error in contract review. By automating the review process, AI can reduce the risk of errors and oversights that can lead to costly legal disputes.

However, there are also some potential challenges and limitations of AI in contract review. One of the main challenges is the need for high-quality data. AI algorithms rely on large volumes of high-quality data to effectively analyze contracts and extract relevant information. If the data is incomplete, inaccurate, or outdated, the results of the analysis may be unreliable.

Another challenge is the potential for bias in AI algorithms. AI is only as unbiased as the data it is trained on, and if the data used to train the algorithm is biased, the results of the analysis may also be biased. This can have serious implications for contract review, as biased analysis could lead to erroneous conclusions and costly legal disputes.

In conclusion, AI has the potential to significantly impact the contract review industry by increasing efficiency, accuracy, and providing valuable insights into contract data. However, it is important to be aware of the potential challenges and limitations of AI and ensure that the data used to train the algorithms is of high quality and unbiased.

Potential Challenges and Limitations of AI in Contract Review

Artificial intelligence (AI) has brought significant advancements in various fields, including contract review. However, like any other technology, AI also has limitations and challenges in contract review.

One of the potential challenges is the quality and quantity of data. AI systems rely on large amounts of data to learn and improve their performance. Therefore, the quality and quantity of data available for training the system can significantly affect its accuracy and efficiency. In contract review, the availability of quality data can be a significant challenge, especially when dealing with unstructured data or documents with inconsistent formatting. Additionally, there can be a lack of standardized data and domain-specific knowledge required for training the AI models.

Another challenge is the complexity of contract language. Legal contracts are often written in complex and specialized language, which can be challenging for AI models to understand and interpret accurately. Ambiguity in the contract language can also pose a challenge as it can result in different interpretations by different AI models, leading to inconsistencies and errors in contract review.

Moreover, AI models may not always consider the context and intent of the contract clauses. For instance, an AI system may flag a clause as non-compliant without considering its intended purpose or the broader context of the contract. This can lead to unnecessary delays and errors in contract review and potentially result in legal disputes.

Another limitation of AI in contract review is the lack of transparency and explainability of the AI models' decision-making processes. Due to the complex nature of AI algorithms, it can be challenging to understand how the models arrive at their decisions. This lack of transparency and explainability can be a significant issue in the legal industry, where accountability and transparency are critical.

In conclusion, while AI has brought significant advancements in contract review, it also has its limitations and challenges. Quality and quantity of data, complexity of contract language, context and intent, and lack of transparency and explainability are some of the potential challenges and limitations of AI in contract review. It is essential to address these challenges to ensure the accurate and efficient use of AI in contract review.

Chapter 3: AI and Predictive Analytics in Law
Overview of Predictive Analytics and Machine Learning Algorithms for Legal Predictions

Predictive analytics and machine learning algorithms have revolutionized the legal industry in recent years. These tools have made it possible to predict the outcomes of legal cases, identify potential risks, and offer insights into how legal decisions might impact business outcomes. In this chapter, we will explore the most common predictive analytics and machine learning algorithms used in the legal industry and discuss how they are used to make legal predictions.

Machine learning is a subfield of artificial intelligence that involves training algorithms to learn from data. Predictive analytics, on the other hand, involves using data, statistical algorithms, and machine learning techniques to identify the likelihood of future outcomes based on historical data. These techniques can be used to predict a variety of legal outcomes, such as the likelihood of winning a case or the amount of damages that might be awarded.

One of the most common types of machine learning algorithms used in legal predictions is supervised learning. Supervised learning involves training an algorithm on labeled data, where the outcome is known, and using that data to predict outcomes for new, unlabeled data. For example, an algorithm could be trained on a dataset of past court cases and their outcomes, and then used to predict the outcome of a new case.

Another popular technique is natural language processing (NLP), which involves teaching algorithms to understand and analyze human language. NLP algorithms can be used to analyze legal documents, such as contracts or court filings, to identify key terms and patterns. This can be useful for predicting the outcome of legal cases, as well as for identifying potential risks in contracts.

In addition to supervised learning and NLP, there are many other machine learning techniques used in legal predictions, such as decision trees, neural networks, and support vector machines. Each of these techniques has its strengths and weaknesses, and the choice of which technique to use depends on the specific problem being addressed.

Overall, predictive analytics and machine learning algorithms have the potential to significantly improve the legal industry by providing insights and predictions that were previously unavailable. However, these tools also come with challenges and limitations that must be addressed. In the next sections, we will explore these challenges and limitations in more detail.

Benefits of Predictive Analytics for the Legal Industry

Predictive analytics has already proved its worth in various industries, such as finance and healthcare, and the legal industry is no exception. Here are some of the benefits of using predictive analytics in the legal industry:

1. Improved decision-making: Predictive analytics can help lawyers make informed decisions by providing them with accurate predictions based on historical data. For instance, predictive analytics can help lawyers predict the outcome of a case or the likelihood of a settlement, which can inform their strategy.

2. Cost savings: Predictive analytics can help law firms save costs by automating tasks and reducing the need for manual review. For instance, by using predictive analytics to review contracts, lawyers can save time and resources that would otherwise have been spent on manual review.

3. Increased efficiency: Predictive analytics can help lawyers work more efficiently by automating repetitive tasks, such as document review. By automating these tasks, lawyers can focus on more complex tasks that require human expertise.

4. Improved accuracy: Predictive analytics can provide lawyers with more accurate predictions than manual

methods. By analyzing large volumes of data, predictive analytics can identify patterns and make predictions that humans might have missed.

5. Competitive advantage: Law firms that adopt predictive analytics early can gain a competitive advantage by offering clients more accurate predictions and better insights. Clients are increasingly demanding more transparency and predictability from their lawyers, and firms that can provide this will be more attractive.

6. Better risk management: Predictive analytics can help lawyers manage risk by identifying potential issues before they become a problem. For instance, predictive analytics can help identify high-risk contracts or potential compliance issues, allowing lawyers to take action before the issue escalates.

Overall, predictive analytics can provide lawyers with valuable insights that can inform their strategy, reduce costs, improve efficiency, and provide a competitive advantage. As such, it's no surprise that predictive analytics is becoming an increasingly important tool in the legal industry.

Predictive analytics and machine learning algorithms have numerous applications in the legal industry. Some of the most promising use cases for these technologies include:

1. Early Case Assessment: Predictive analytics can help lawyers evaluate the strength of a case early on. By analyzing patterns in historical data, algorithms can predict the likelihood of a case's success and identify key factors that influence outcomes.

2. Contract Management: Predictive analytics can be used to analyze contracts and identify potential risks and opportunities. For example, an algorithm can automatically flag clauses that may be problematic or require further negotiation.

3. Litigation Analysis: Predictive analytics can help lawyers assess the potential outcomes of litigation. By analyzing historical data, algorithms can identify patterns in judge and jury decisions and predict the likelihood of success in a particular case.

4. Risk Assessment: Predictive analytics can be used to assess risk in various legal contexts, such as mergers and acquisitions, regulatory compliance, and intellectual property protection. By analyzing data on past cases and

regulatory decisions, algorithms can help lawyers identify potential risks and take proactive measures to mitigate them.

5. E-Discovery: Predictive analytics can help lawyers streamline the e-discovery process by automatically identifying relevant documents and flagging those that are likely to be privileged or confidential.

6. Sentencing and Parole: Predictive analytics can be used to assess the likelihood of recidivism and guide sentencing and parole decisions. By analyzing data on past offenders and their outcomes, algorithms can identify patterns and risk factors that may influence future behavior.

7. Legal Research: Predictive analytics can be used to improve legal research by predicting the relevance of cases and documents to a particular query. By analyzing patterns in historical data, algorithms can identify the most relevant cases and prioritize them for review.

8. Intellectual Property: Predictive analytics can help lawyers assess the strength of a patent or trademark by analyzing data on past decisions and identifying patterns that may influence the outcome of a case.

9. Compliance Monitoring: Predictive analytics can be used to monitor compliance with various legal and regulatory requirements. By analyzing data on past violations and enforcement actions, algorithms can identify

patterns and potential risks and help companies take proactive measures to avoid future violations.

10. Fraud Detection: Predictive analytics can be used to detect and prevent fraud in various legal contexts, such as insurance claims and financial transactions. By analyzing patterns in data, algorithms can identify potential fraudulent activity and alert lawyers and investigators to take action.

Overall, predictive analytics and machine learning algorithms have the potential to revolutionize the legal industry by providing lawyers with powerful tools to analyze data, assess risks, and make better-informed decisions. However, there are also challenges and limitations to consider, including issues related to data privacy, bias, and ethical considerations. It is essential for lawyers and legal professionals to be aware of these challenges and work to address them as the use of AI in the legal industry continues to grow.

Potential Ethical Implications of Predictive Analytics in Law

Predictive analytics, powered by machine learning algorithms, can offer significant benefits to the legal industry by enabling lawyers to make more informed decisions based on data analysis. However, as with any technology, there are also potential ethical implications that must be considered. In this section, we will explore some of the potential ethical implications of predictive analytics in law.

1. Bias in Data and Algorithms Predictive analytics relies on data and algorithms to make predictions about the future. However, if the data used to train the algorithm is biased, the algorithm will also be biased. This can lead to unfair or discriminatory outcomes, particularly in areas such as criminal justice, where predictive analytics is being used to make decisions about bail, sentencing, and parole. It is therefore essential that legal professionals are aware of the potential for bias in the data and algorithms they use and take steps to minimize it.

2. Transparency and Explainability Another potential ethical concern with predictive analytics in law is the lack of transparency and explainability in the algorithms used. When a decision is made based on predictive analytics, it can be difficult to understand how the algorithm arrived at that

decision. This lack of transparency can make it difficult for individuals to challenge decisions made using predictive analytics and can erode trust in the legal system. To address this concern, some experts have called for greater transparency and explainability in the algorithms used for predictive analytics in law.

3. Privacy and Data Security Predictive analytics relies on data, and the use of this data can raise concerns about privacy and data security. Legal professionals must ensure that any data used for predictive analytics is collected and used in compliance with relevant data protection laws and regulations. Additionally, they must take appropriate measures to protect the data from unauthorized access or disclosure, including ensuring that any third-party service providers involved in the process are also compliant with relevant data protection laws and regulations.

4. Reliance on Algorithms Finally, there is a concern that the use of predictive analytics in law could lead to a reliance on algorithms over human judgment. While algorithms can be useful tools for decision-making, they should not replace the judgment of experienced legal professionals. Legal professionals must ensure that they are using predictive analytics as a tool to support their decision-making, rather than relying on it completely.

In conclusion, predictive analytics has the potential to revolutionize the legal industry by enabling lawyers to make more informed decisions based on data analysis. However, it is important to recognize and address the potential ethical implications of this technology, including bias in data and algorithms, lack of transparency and explainability, privacy and data security concerns, and the potential overreliance on algorithms over human judgment. By taking a thoughtful and proactive approach to these concerns, legal professionals can ensure that predictive analytics is used in a responsible and ethical manner.

Artificial Intelligence (AI) is revolutionizing intellectual property (IP) law in many ways. AI applications are enhancing the speed and accuracy of IP searches, automating routine tasks, and improving the efficiency of the IP registration process. Some of the AI applications in IP law include:

1. Prior Art Searches: Prior art search is an essential component of the patent application process. AI-powered search tools can be used to identify relevant prior art, including patents, patent applications, and non-patent literature, with greater speed and accuracy. By utilizing natural language processing (NLP) and machine learning (ML) algorithms, these tools can identify prior art that may have been missed by traditional search methods.

2. Patent Drafting: AI can assist in drafting patent applications by generating summaries of technical papers and identifying similar patents that can help guide the drafting process. AI algorithms can also help identify potential infringement risks and suggest possible workarounds.

3. Patent Prosecution: AI can be used to analyze patent claims and identify potential rejections before they

are issued. This can help patent attorneys prepare more effective responses to office actions and save time and money for clients.

4. Trademark Searches: AI-powered search tools can also be used to search for trademarks that may conflict with existing trademarks. These tools can help identify similar trademarks and provide information on the likelihood of a successful registration.

Benefits of AI Applications in Intellectual Property Law

The benefits of using AI in IP law are numerous. Some of the key benefits include:

1. Increased Efficiency: By automating routine tasks such as prior art searches, AI can save time and increase efficiency. This can result in faster and more accurate results, which can help clients save money and get patents approved more quickly.

2. Improved Accuracy: AI-powered search tools can identify prior art and trademarks that may have been missed by traditional search methods. This can help clients avoid costly infringement lawsuits and ensure that their patents are valid.

3. Cost Savings: By automating routine tasks and increasing efficiency, AI can help reduce costs for clients.

This can make IP services more accessible to smaller companies and startups that may not have the resources to invest in traditional IP services.

4. Increased Access to Information: AI-powered search tools can provide access to a larger volume of information than traditional search methods. This can help clients identify relevant prior art and trademarks that may have been missed by traditional search methods.

Legal Use Cases for AI in Intellectual Property Law

AI can be used in many areas of IP law. Some of the key legal use cases for AI in IP law include:

1. Patent Search and Analysis: AI-powered search tools can be used to conduct prior art searches and analyze patents to identify infringement risks and potential workarounds.

2. Patent Drafting: AI can assist in drafting patent applications by generating summaries of technical papers and identifying similar patents that can help guide the drafting process.

3. Patent Prosecution: AI can be used to analyze patent claims and identify potential rejections before they are issued. This can help patent attorneys prepare more effective responses to office actions.

4. Trademark Searches: AI-powered search tools can be used to search for trademarks that may conflict with existing trademarks. These tools can help identify similar trademarks and provide information on the likelihood of a successful registration.

5. Copyright Protection: AI can be used to identify copyrighted content and help prevent infringement. This can be particularly useful in the digital age, where copyrighted content can be easily distributed and shared online.

Potential Challenges and Limitations of AI in Intellectual Property Law

While AI applications have many potential benefits for IP law, there are also some challenges and limitations that must be considered. Some of these challenges include the potential for errors in data analysis, bias in machine learning algorithms, and the lack of interpretability and transparency in AI decision-making processes. In addition, there are concerns regarding the protection of sensitive information and data privacy in the use of AI in IP law. Despite these challenges, however, AI has the potential to revolutionize the way IP law is practiced and offer new opportunities for innovation and creativity.

One such opportunity is the use of AI in patent analysis and search. The process of conducting a patent search can be time-consuming and costly for lawyers and inventors. However, AI-assisted patent search can significantly reduce the time and effort needed to find relevant prior art and identify potential patent infringement. AI can also assist in patent drafting by generating automated descriptions of inventions and predicting the likelihood of patent approval based on past trends and data. Additionally, AI can aid in trademark registration and enforcement by conducting automated trademark searches and monitoring for potential infringement.

AI-generated Inventions and Patent Law

The use of AI in the innovation process has led to the creation of new inventions that were previously not possible. AI-generated inventions refer to novel and non-obvious inventions that have been entirely or significantly developed by AI without human intervention. These inventions can be a result of machine learning algorithms that identify patterns or correlations in vast data sets, leading to a novel invention or a new use for an existing invention.

The question that arises is who should own the rights to these AI-generated inventions, and what implications do they have for patent law? The current legal framework surrounding patent law is designed for human inventors, and there is no clear legal guidance on how to deal with AI-generated inventions. Some countries, such as the UK and the EU, have recently introduced legislation to address this issue. In the UK, for example, the Intellectual Property Office has stated that an AI inventor cannot be named as an inventor, but the person or organization that owns the AI system that generated the invention can be named as the inventor.

Another issue that arises with AI-generated inventions is the question of whether they are eligible for patent protection. Patent law requires an invention to be novel, non-obvious, and useful. The novelty requirement can be problematic for AI-generated inventions since the AI system may have generated the invention based on existing data, which may not be known to the inventor. Moreover, the non-obvious requirement can also be challenging since the AI system may have identified an invention that would not have been obvious to a human inventor. As a result, there is a need to develop new legal frameworks that can accommodate AI-generated inventions and ensure that patent law remains relevant in the age of AI.

Despite the legal challenges surrounding AI-generated inventions, the use of AI in the patent application process has several benefits. AI can assist patent attorneys in performing prior art searches and conducting patentability assessments. AI can also help patent attorneys identify potential infringers and assess the validity of patents. In addition, AI can help inventors identify the patentability of their inventions by analyzing vast amounts of data and identifying patterns and correlations that may not be apparent to human inventors.

In conclusion, AI-generated inventions are transforming the innovation landscape, and their impact on patent law is significant. The legal framework surrounding patent law needs to adapt to ensure that AI-generated inventions are adequately protected while also addressing the ethical and legal implications of AI in the innovation process.

AI-generated content, also known as computer-generated content (CGC), refers to the text, images, or other media produced by an AI algorithm. As AI technology continues to advance, the amount of content generated by these algorithms is increasing rapidly. While this has many potential benefits, such as the ability to generate personalized content quickly and at scale, it also raises several legal issues that need to be addressed.

One of the main legal issues surrounding AI-generated content is copyright. Under copyright law, the creator of a work is typically the owner of the copyright. However, with AI-generated content, it may not always be clear who the creator is. If a human creates an algorithm that generates content, the human would likely be the creator and own the copyright. However, if an AI algorithm creates content autonomously, without any human input or intervention, it is not clear who should be considered the creator.

This issue was brought to the forefront in 2018 when a group of researchers created an AI algorithm that could generate realistic-looking portraits. The researchers attempted to sell these portraits as unique works of art, but they were quickly challenged by an artist who claimed that the AI-generated portraits were copies of her own work. The legal case that followed raised questions about whether an AI algorithm could be considered a legal author under copyright law.

Another legal issue surrounding AI-generated content is the potential for defamation or libel. If an AI algorithm generates content that is defamatory or libelous, it may not be clear who is responsible for the content. In traditional media, the author or publisher of the content is typically held responsible for any defamatory statements. However, with AI-generated content, it is not clear who should be held responsible if the algorithm generates defamatory content autonomously.

In addition to these legal issues, there are also ethical concerns surrounding AI-generated content. Some critics argue that the use of AI to generate content could lead to a loss of creativity and diversity, as algorithms may favor certain styles or subjects over others. There are also concerns about the potential for AI-generated content to be used to spread misinformation or propaganda, as algorithms can be programmed to generate content that supports a particular viewpoint or agenda.

Overall, the legal issues surrounding AI-generated content are complex and multifaceted. As AI technology continues to advance, it will be important for lawmakers and legal experts to develop new frameworks and guidelines to address these issues and ensure that the legal and ethical implications of AI-generated content are properly addressed.

Challenges of Regulating AI in Intellectual Property Law

As AI technology continues to advance, there is a growing need for regulations to govern its use, particularly in the realm of intellectual property law. With AI generating content and inventions, it can be difficult to determine who owns the rights to these creations, which creates a legal grey area. This chapter will explore the challenges of regulating AI in intellectual property law and the potential solutions to these challenges.

1. Ownership of AI-Generated Creations:

One of the most significant challenges of regulating AI in intellectual property law is determining who owns the rights to AI-generated creations. For example, if an AI system generates a new invention, who owns the patent for that invention? Does the ownership belong to the person who created the AI system, the person who trained the AI system, or the AI system itself? There is currently no clear legal precedent for this, and it is unclear how this issue will be resolved.

2. Copyright Infringement:

AI can generate content that is similar or identical to existing works, which raises the issue of copyright infringement. For example, if an AI system generates a new song that is identical to an existing song, who owns the rights to the new song? This issue becomes more complex when the AI system is trained on copyrighted works, making it difficult to determine whether the AI-generated content is original or a derivative work.

3. Ethical Issues:

Regulating AI in intellectual property law raises ethical concerns, particularly when it comes to AI-generated content. For example, if an AI system generates a news article or a social media post, it can be difficult to determine whether the content is biased or contains false information. This raises the question of who is responsible for the content generated by the AI system.

4. Lack of Regulation:

Another challenge of regulating AI in intellectual property law is the lack of regulation. As AI technology continues to advance, it is becoming increasingly difficult to keep up with the technology and regulate its use. This lack of regulation creates uncertainty and makes it difficult for individuals and organizations to determine their legal rights and obligations.

Potential Solutions:

1. Establishing Clear Legal Frameworks:

To address the challenges of regulating AI in intellectual property law, clear legal frameworks must be established. These frameworks should address issues such as ownership of AI-generated creations, copyright infringement, and ethical concerns.

2. Implementing AI-Specific Regulations:

AI-specific regulations should be implemented to govern the use of AI in intellectual property law. These regulations should be tailored to the unique challenges posed by AI technology and should be regularly updated to keep pace with advances in AI.

3. Encouraging Collaboration Between Legal and Technical Experts:

Collaboration between legal and technical experts is essential to developing effective regulations for AI in intellectual property law. Legal experts can provide guidance on legal issues, while technical experts can provide insights into the capabilities and limitations of AI technology.

Conclusion:

Regulating AI in intellectual property law poses significant challenges, but it is essential to ensuring that the legal rights of individuals and organizations are protected. Clear legal frameworks, AI-specific regulations, and collaboration between legal and technical experts are critical to developing effective regulations for AI in intellectual property law. With the right approach, it is possible to harness the power of AI technology while protecting the legal rights of all parties involved.

Chapter 5: AI and E-Discovery
AI-assisted E-Discovery

AI-assisted e-discovery is a process of using AI technologies to help legal professionals in the discovery phase of a lawsuit. This process involves collecting, processing, and reviewing electronic documents and data to identify relevant information that can be used as evidence in a case. E-discovery is a critical step in litigation, as it can help lawyers to establish the facts of a case, assess the strengths and weaknesses of their client's position, and develop strategies for trial.

One of the main advantages of AI-assisted e-discovery is its ability to automate repetitive tasks that are time-consuming and error-prone when done manually. For example, AI tools can quickly and accurately identify relevant documents from a large pool of data, eliminating the need for lawyers to manually review each document. AI can also classify documents by relevance, privilege, and other criteria, making it easier for lawyers to quickly identify key pieces of evidence.

Another benefit of AI-assisted e-discovery is its ability to handle large volumes of data. With the increasing amount of electronic data available, traditional e-discovery methods can quickly become overwhelming and inefficient. AI tools, on the other hand, can process vast amounts of data in a short period of time, allowing lawyers to quickly identify important information.

AI technologies can also help improve the accuracy of e-discovery by reducing the risk of human error. AI can detect patterns in data that might be missed by a human reviewer and can ensure that all relevant information is identified and considered. By eliminating errors and omissions, AI can help lawyers to build stronger cases and make more informed decisions.

Overall, AI-assisted e-discovery can provide significant benefits to the legal profession, including increased efficiency, accuracy, and cost savings. As AI technologies continue to evolve and improve, e-discovery will become even more streamlined and effective, allowing lawyers to focus on building the strongest possible cases for their clients.

The use of AI in e-discovery has several advantages over traditional methods. Some of the most common use cases for AI in e-discovery include:

1. Early case assessment: One of the most important stages of e-discovery is early case assessment (ECA). AI tools can quickly analyze data to identify key documents, reduce the data set to be reviewed, and even identify potential case outcomes. This can save a significant amount of time and reduce the costs associated with e-discovery.

2. Document classification and clustering: AI tools can analyze documents and group them into clusters based on their content, language, metadata, and other features. This helps to identify relevant documents more quickly, reduce the number of irrelevant documents that need to be reviewed, and improve the overall accuracy of the review process.

3. Email threading: AI tools can identify and group related email threads, allowing reviewers to more easily follow conversations and identify relevant information.

4. Concept searching: AI tools can analyze the content of documents and identify related concepts, allowing reviewers to identify additional relevant documents that may not have been found through keyword searches.

5. Predictive coding: Predictive coding, also known as technology-assisted review (TAR), uses machine learning algorithms to classify documents as either relevant or irrelevant based on a sample set of documents that have already been reviewed. This can significantly reduce the time and costs associated with manual document review.

6. Redaction: AI tools can automatically redact sensitive information from documents, such as personal identifying information, before they are produced in discovery.

7. Audio and video analysis: AI tools can analyze audio and video recordings to identify relevant content, such as keywords, topics, and sentiment.

8. Compliance monitoring: AI tools can monitor corporate communications and data to identify potential compliance violations, such as insider trading or data breaches.

These use cases demonstrate how AI can significantly improve the efficiency and accuracy of e-discovery. However, it is important to note that AI is not a silver bullet and there are limitations and challenges to its implementation in e-discovery.

Impact of AI on E-Discovery Industry

The use of AI in e-discovery has significant implications for the legal industry. Here are some ways in which AI is changing the e-discovery industry:

1. Increased Efficiency: AI-powered e-discovery tools are designed to sift through large amounts of data in a matter of hours or days, as opposed to weeks or months. By automating the review process, legal professionals can quickly identify relevant information and expedite the discovery process.

2. Reduced Costs: With AI-powered e-discovery tools, legal teams can save significant amounts of money on discovery-related costs. Automated processes reduce the need for manual review, thereby reducing the hours spent by legal teams on a review and ultimately the cost.

3. Improved Accuracy: AI-powered e-discovery tools can help improve the accuracy of document review. By using machine learning algorithms to identify patterns and relevance, legal professionals can identify relevant information more quickly and accurately than they would be able to do manually.

4. Predictive Coding: One of the key features of AI-powered e-discovery tools is predictive coding. This allows legal professionals to train the AI system to identify relevant

documents based on their coding, which can then be applied to the remaining documents. Predictive coding can significantly reduce the time and cost associated with document review.

5. Increased Consistency: AI-powered e-discovery tools offer consistency and standardization in document review, ensuring that each document is reviewed in the same way, regardless of the reviewer. This reduces the risk of errors and inconsistencies that can arise from human reviewers.

6. New Opportunities: The use of AI-powered e-discovery tools has created new opportunities for legal professionals, particularly in the area of data analytics. By analyzing large amounts of data, legal professionals can identify trends and patterns that can help them better understand the legal landscape and improve their legal strategies.

7. Faster Case Resolutions: With AI-powered e-discovery tools, legal professionals can quickly identify relevant information, which can lead to faster case resolutions. This can help reduce the time and costs associated with legal disputes, ultimately benefiting clients.

Overall, the use of AI in e-discovery is transforming the legal industry, making the discovery process more efficient, accurate, and cost-effective. As AI-powered e-discovery tools continue to evolve, legal professionals will be able to leverage them to provide even more value to their clients.

Potential Challenges and Limitations of AI in E-Discovery

AI has the potential to transform the e-discovery process, but there are also some challenges and limitations that must be considered. Some of the key challenges and limitations include:

1. Bias in AI algorithms: Like all machine learning models, AI algorithms used in e-discovery can be biased. The bias can be introduced during the training phase or through the data used to develop the algorithm. This bias can result in the exclusion of relevant documents or the inclusion of irrelevant documents, leading to incorrect outcomes.

2. Lack of transparency: AI algorithms can be complex, making it difficult to understand how they work and why they produce certain results. This lack of transparency can make it difficult to challenge the results in court.

3. Cost: While AI can help reduce the cost of e-discovery, the initial investment in AI technology and the cost of training and maintaining the AI system can be significant.

4. Security and privacy concerns: The use of AI in e-discovery requires access to sensitive data. There is a risk

that this data could be accessed or stolen by hackers, leading to serious security and privacy concerns.

5. Limited applicability: AI algorithms may not be suitable for all types of e-discovery cases. Some cases may require a more human-driven approach, particularly where there is a high level of complexity or ambiguity.

6. Need for human expertise: While AI can help automate many aspects of e-discovery, human expertise is still required to ensure that the results are accurate and relevant. Human reviewers are necessary to validate the results and make any necessary adjustments.

7. Regulatory and ethical issues: The use of AI in e-discovery raises important ethical and regulatory issues. There is a need for clear guidelines and regulations to ensure that AI is used in a responsible and ethical manner.

In conclusion, while AI has the potential to improve the efficiency and accuracy of e-discovery, there are also several challenges and limitations that must be considered. It is important to carefully evaluate the benefits and risks of using AI in e-discovery and to develop strategies to address any potential challenges and limitations. By doing so, organizations can effectively leverage the power of AI to streamline the e-discovery process and achieve better outcomes.

Chapter 6: AI and Legal Writing

AI-assisted Legal Writing

AI technology is increasingly being used in the legal industry to help with legal writing. While AI cannot replace human lawyers, it can help with some aspects of legal writing and improve efficiency. This section will discuss AI-assisted legal writing, including the benefits, use cases, and potential limitations.

Benefits of AI-Assisted Legal Writing

One of the main benefits of AI-assisted legal writing is efficiency. AI can analyze large amounts of data and provide insights into patterns and trends that may not be immediately apparent to a human writer. This can help lawyers save time and make more informed decisions.

AI can also assist with accuracy and consistency in legal writing. AI can catch errors, inconsistencies, and potential issues in legal documents, which can help to avoid mistakes and reduce the risk of litigation. By ensuring that legal documents are accurate and consistent, AI can help to improve the quality of legal work and enhance the reputation of law firms.

Use Cases for AI-Assisted Legal Writing

There are many potential use cases for AI-assisted legal writing, including:

1. Contract drafting: AI can be used to help draft contracts by providing suggestions for clauses and highlighting potential issues. This can help lawyers to draft contracts more efficiently and accurately.

2. Legal research: AI can help with legal research by analyzing large amounts of data and providing insights into patterns and trends. This can help lawyers to make more informed decisions and provide better advice to clients.

3. Brief writing: AI can help with brief writing by analyzing relevant cases and providing suggestions for arguments. This can help lawyers to draft more persuasive briefs and improve their chances of winning cases.

4. Compliance: AI can be used to help with compliance by analyzing regulations and providing suggestions for compliance strategies. This can help companies to stay up-to-date with regulations and avoid potential legal issues.

Potential Limitations of AI-Assisted Legal Writing

While AI-assisted legal writing has many potential benefits, there are also some limitations that must be considered. One of the main limitations is the potential for bias. AI algorithms are only as good as the data they are trained on, and if the data is biased, the AI may produce biased results.

Another potential limitation is the lack of human judgment. While AI can provide insights and suggestions, it cannot replace the judgment and experience of a human lawyer. This means that AI should be used as a tool to assist lawyers, rather than as a replacement for them.

Finally, there are concerns about the potential loss of jobs as a result of AI-assisted legal writing. While AI can improve efficiency and reduce the time required for certain tasks, it is unlikely to completely replace human lawyers. However, there may be a shift in the types of tasks that lawyers perform, which could result in some job losses.

Conclusion

AI-assisted legal writing has the potential to improve efficiency, accuracy, and consistency in legal work. While there are some potential limitations and challenges, the benefits of AI in legal writing cannot be ignored. As AI technology continues to evolve, it will become increasingly important for lawyers and law firms to embrace this technology and incorporate it into their work.

Natural Language Generation and Machine Learning for Legal Writing

Natural language generation (NLG) is a technology that uses machine learning algorithms to automatically generate natural-sounding language based on data input. In the legal industry, NLG has the potential to transform legal writing by automating the drafting of legal documents and contracts, simplifying complex legal language, and improving communication between lawyers and clients.

One use case of NLG in legal writing is contract drafting. Lawyers can use NLG software to input the necessary legal terms and provisions, and the software can generate a complete contract in natural language. This not only saves time and reduces errors, but it also makes legal documents more accessible to non-lawyers who may struggle with understanding legal jargon.

Another use case is legal briefs and memos. Lawyers can input the relevant facts and legal arguments, and the NLG software can generate a comprehensive and persuasive brief or memo. This can help lawyers meet tight deadlines and reduce the workload of legal staff.

Machine learning algorithms can also improve legal writing by analyzing large amounts of legal data and predicting outcomes in similar cases. By analyzing previous cases and court decisions, machine learning algorithms can help lawyers identify key arguments and evidence to support their case.

In addition, machine learning algorithms can improve legal writing by identifying errors in grammar, syntax, and spelling. This can help lawyers produce higher quality documents and reduce the risk of errors and omissions.

Overall, NLG and machine learning algorithms have the potential to transform legal writing by automating the drafting of legal documents, simplifying complex legal language, and improving communication between lawyers and clients. By reducing the time and effort required to produce legal documents, lawyers can focus on more strategic tasks and provide better value to their clients.

Impact of AI on Legal Writing Industry

AI is having a significant impact on the legal writing industry. With the ability to analyze vast amounts of data, AI tools can generate insights that were previously impossible to uncover. This has led to increased efficiency, accuracy, and speed in the legal writing process. Here are some ways in which AI is impacting the legal writing industry:

1. Increased Efficiency: AI tools can review documents and extract relevant information much faster than humans. For example, natural language processing (NLP) algorithms can quickly scan through legal documents to identify key concepts and topics, reducing the time it takes to conduct legal research. This allows lawyers to focus on higher-level tasks and ultimately results in increased productivity.

2. Improved Accuracy: AI tools can help improve the accuracy of legal writing. For instance, machine learning algorithms can be trained on vast amounts of legal data to predict the outcome of a case with a high degree of accuracy. This means that lawyers can make more informed decisions based on data-driven insights, resulting in better outcomes for their clients.

3. Enhanced Personalization: AI can also be used to personalize legal writing. For example, chatbots and other conversational AI tools can be used to generate responses to

common legal questions in real-time, providing personalized advice to clients. This enhances the client experience and helps build trust and loyalty.

4. Access to New Data Sources: AI tools can also be used to analyze unstructured data sources, such as social media and news articles, to identify emerging legal issues and trends. This can help lawyers stay ahead of the curve and provide proactive advice to clients.

5. Creation of New Business Models: AI is also creating new business models in the legal writing industry. For example, some companies are using AI-powered tools to automate the creation of legal documents, such as contracts and agreements. This can significantly reduce costs and speed up the document creation process, making legal services more accessible to a wider range of clients.

Despite the numerous benefits of AI in the legal writing industry, there are also some challenges that must be considered.

1. Integration with Existing Systems: Integrating AI tools with existing legal systems and processes can be challenging. Legal organizations must ensure that their AI tools are compatible with their existing systems and workflows.

2. Security and Privacy Concerns: The use of AI in legal writing raises concerns about data privacy and security. Lawyers must ensure that sensitive client data is protected and that their AI tools are compliant with relevant data protection laws.

3. Ethical Considerations: The use of AI in legal writing also raises ethical considerations, such as bias and accountability. Legal organizations must ensure that their AI tools are transparent, accountable, and free from bias.

4. Impact on the Legal Workforce: AI tools are likely to change the nature of legal work, potentially resulting in job losses or changes in the skills required for legal work. Legal organizations must ensure that their workforce is equipped with the skills required to work alongside AI tools.

Overall, AI is transforming the legal writing industry by enhancing efficiency, accuracy, and personalization. While there are challenges that must be considered, the benefits of AI in legal writing are likely to continue to grow as the technology advances.

Potential Challenges and Limitations of AI in Legal Writing

AI-assisted legal writing has the potential to revolutionize the legal industry by making it faster and more efficient. However, like any technology, there are also potential challenges and limitations that must be considered.

One challenge is the accuracy of the AI-generated text. While AI algorithms can generate text quickly, there is a risk of errors and inaccuracies. These errors can have serious consequences, particularly in legal writing where precision and clarity are essential. To mitigate this risk, it is important to train AI algorithms using large datasets of accurate legal text and to develop techniques for verifying the accuracy of AI-generated text.

Another challenge is the potential for bias in AI-generated text. AI algorithms learn from the data they are trained on, and if that data is biased, the algorithm will reproduce that bias in its output. In the legal context, this can be particularly problematic if the bias affects decisions made by judges, juries, or other legal professionals. To address this issue, it is important to carefully select and review the data used to train AI algorithms, and to develop techniques for detecting and correcting bias in AI-generated text.

Another potential limitation is the inability of AI algorithms to fully capture the nuances of human language and reasoning. Legal writing often requires the ability to understand and apply complex legal concepts, and to interpret the meaning and intent behind written language. While AI algorithms can assist with certain aspects of legal writing, such as generating boilerplate language and identifying relevant legal precedents, they may struggle with more nuanced tasks such as drafting legal arguments or interpreting the intent of a contract provision.

Finally, there is also the risk of AI-generated text being used to replace human legal professionals, particularly in areas such as document review and drafting. While AI algorithms can assist with these tasks, they cannot replace the expertise and judgment of human lawyers. In addition, there is a risk that increased reliance on AI-generated text could lead to a loss of jobs in the legal industry, particularly in areas such as paralegal work.

In conclusion, AI-assisted legal writing has the potential to transform the legal industry, but there are also potential challenges and limitations that must be considered. By addressing these challenges and developing strategies for mitigating their impact, we can ensure that AI is used to its fullest potential while also preserving the integrity and expertise of the legal profession.

Chapter 7: AI and the Future of the Legal Industry

The Potential Future of AI in Law

The potential future of AI in the legal industry is vast and expansive, with many experts predicting significant changes in the coming years. Here are some of the ways AI could impact the legal industry in the future:

1. Increased Efficiency: One of the most significant advantages of AI in law is the ability to streamline processes, reduce errors, and increase efficiency. In the future, legal firms are likely to incorporate AI to automate routine tasks, such as contract review and document analysis, freeing up lawyers to focus on more complex legal issues.

2. Enhanced Decision-Making: AI has the potential to augment human decision-making by providing lawyers with valuable insights and recommendations based on large sets of data. As AI becomes more sophisticated, it is likely that legal professionals will use it to make more informed decisions, such as determining the likelihood of success in a case or identifying legal precedents.

3. Improved Access to Justice: AI could play a crucial role in increasing access to justice by making legal services more affordable and accessible to those who cannot afford

traditional legal representation. Chatbots and virtual assistants could provide legal guidance to those who cannot afford a lawyer, and AI-powered tools could simplify legal language and make it easier for individuals to navigate the legal system.

4. Increased Personalization: AI could also help legal professionals provide more personalized services to their clients. By analyzing data on clients' behavior and preferences, AI could enable lawyers to tailor their approach and communication to individual clients, resulting in better outcomes.

5. Cybersecurity: As technology becomes increasingly integral to the legal industry, cybersecurity threats are likely to become more prevalent. AI-powered security solutions could help legal firms protect their clients' confidential information, detect and prevent cyber attacks, and monitor network activity for potential threats.

6. Increased Collaboration: Finally, AI has the potential to facilitate collaboration and knowledge-sharing among legal professionals. Tools such as predictive analytics and natural language processing could help lawyers share information and insights more easily, resulting in more effective legal strategies and better outcomes for clients.

While the potential benefits of AI in law are significant, there are also potential downsides and challenges to consider. For example, the use of AI could exacerbate existing biases in the legal system, and there are concerns around the ethical implications of using AI to make decisions that could impact individuals' rights and freedoms. Additionally, the introduction of AI could lead to job losses in the legal industry, as automation reduces the need for certain roles.

In conclusion, the future of AI in law is complex and multifaceted, with both potential benefits and challenges to consider. While AI is unlikely to replace human lawyers entirely, it has the potential to transform the legal industry and improve outcomes for legal professionals and clients alike. It is up to legal professionals to stay informed about the latest AI developments and consider how they can best leverage this technology to serve their clients' needs.

Impact of AI on the Legal Profession and Legal Education

AI is rapidly transforming the legal industry, from e-discovery and legal writing to predictive analytics and machine learning. As AI continues to develop and improve, it will undoubtedly have a profound impact on the legal profession and legal education.

One of the most significant impacts of AI on the legal profession will be on the nature of legal work. Many of the repetitive, routine tasks currently performed by human lawyers, such as document review and contract analysis, will increasingly be automated by AI. This has the potential to make legal services more efficient and affordable for clients, but it also raises questions about the future of legal jobs.

Some experts predict that AI will lead to a significant reduction in the number of lawyers needed to perform certain tasks, while others argue that AI will simply change the nature of legal work rather than eliminate it altogether. For example, AI may lead to an increased demand for lawyers who are skilled in working with and interpreting AI systems.

In addition to its impact on the legal profession, AI is also likely to have an impact on legal education. Law schools will need to adapt their curricula to prepare students for a legal industry that is increasingly influenced by AI. This may involve teaching students about the technical aspects of AI and how it is used in the legal industry, as well as the ethical considerations surrounding the use of AI in legal practice.

Another potential impact of AI on legal education is the development of new interdisciplinary programs that combine law and technology. These programs could train lawyers to work closely with technologists, data scientists, and other professionals to develop and implement AI systems in the legal industry.

However, there are also potential challenges associated with the impact of AI on the legal profession and legal education. For example, there may be concerns about bias and discrimination in AI systems, which could have significant legal and ethical implications. Additionally, there may be challenges in ensuring that AI systems are transparent and explainable, which is critical for ensuring that they are fair and reliable.

In conclusion, AI is poised to have a significant impact on the legal profession and legal education in the coming years. While there are potential challenges and limitations associated with the use of AI in the legal industry, there are also many exciting opportunities for AI to make legal services more efficient, accessible, and affordable for clients.

As the legal industry continues to evolve, it will be important for lawyers, law schools, and other legal professionals to stay informed about the latest developments in AI and adapt to this rapidly changing landscape.

Ethical Implications of AI in Law

The emergence of artificial intelligence (AI) has brought about significant changes in various industries, including the legal industry. AI technology is transforming the legal profession by enabling faster and more accurate decision-making, enhancing the efficiency of legal services, and expanding access to justice. However, the adoption of AI in the legal profession has also raised several ethical concerns. This section will explore the ethical implications of AI in law, including the potential risks and challenges.

Privacy and Data Protection:

One of the significant ethical concerns with AI in law is the protection of privacy and data. AI systems collect vast amounts of data, which can be used to identify individuals and their behavior patterns. This raises concerns about the potential misuse of such data, as well as the protection of privacy rights. The legal profession must ensure that AI systems comply with data protection laws and ethical standards.

Bias and Discrimination:

Another ethical issue with AI in law is the potential for bias and discrimination. AI systems rely on algorithms that are trained on historical data, which may contain biases and reflect societal prejudices. As a result, AI systems may perpetuate existing inequalities and prejudices, leading to discriminatory outcomes. The legal profession must ensure that AI systems are transparent, explainable, and auditable to detect and correct any biases that may arise.

Accountability and Liability:

AI systems raise questions about accountability and liability. Who is responsible for the actions and decisions of AI systems? Is it the developer, the user, or the AI system itself? This raises concerns about the potential for harm caused by AI systems and the need for clear guidelines on liability and accountability. The legal profession must ensure that AI systems are designed to be accountable and transparent, and that there are clear guidelines on liability for harm caused by AI systems.

Professional Ethics:

AI in law raises concerns about professional ethics. For instance, lawyers have an ethical obligation to provide independent and unbiased legal advice to their clients. However, the use of AI systems in legal services may raise conflicts of interest and threaten the independence of lawyers. The legal profession must ensure that the use of AI systems does not compromise professional ethics, and that lawyers are trained on the ethical use of AI systems.

Conclusion:

AI technology has the potential to transform the legal industry, but it also raises several ethical concerns. The legal profession must address these concerns to ensure that AI systems are developed, deployed, and used ethically. The protection of privacy and data, the prevention of bias and discrimination, accountability and liability, and professional ethics are some of the key ethical concerns that must be addressed. By addressing these concerns, the legal profession can leverage the benefits of AI technology while ensuring that it is used ethically and responsibly.

Opportunities and Challenges for the Legal Industry in the Age of AI

Introduction Artificial intelligence (AI) has been transforming the legal industry in recent years, creating new opportunities and challenges for legal professionals. In this section, we will explore the potential opportunities and challenges that AI presents for the legal industry, including the impact on legal practice, the role of lawyers, and legal education.

Opportunities for the Legal Industry in the Age of AI

1. Increased Efficiency and Productivity One of the most significant benefits of AI for the legal industry is its ability to automate routine and repetitive tasks, freeing up lawyers' time to focus on higher-value tasks. AI-powered tools such as document review and contract analysis software can process large volumes of data much faster and more accurately than human lawyers. This increased efficiency can lead to cost savings for clients and law firms and can also increase the productivity of lawyers.

2. Enhanced Decision Making AI can also help lawyers make better-informed decisions by providing them with relevant information and insights. For example, predictive analytics can help lawyers predict case outcomes, which can inform case strategy and settlement negotiations.

AI-powered research tools can also help lawyers find relevant case law and legal precedent quickly and easily, improving the quality and accuracy of legal research.

3. Improved Access to Justice AI can also help improve access to justice by making legal services more affordable and accessible. Chatbots and virtual assistants can provide legal guidance to individuals who cannot afford a lawyer or who live in remote areas without access to legal services. AI-powered tools can also help lawyers provide more affordable and efficient legal services to their clients, reducing the cost and time required to complete legal tasks.

4. New Business Models AI is also creating new business models for the legal industry. For example, some law firms are using AI-powered contract analysis tools to offer fixed-fee services to their clients. This allows clients to know upfront how much their legal services will cost, providing greater transparency and predictability.

Challenges for the Legal Industry in the Age of AI

1. Job Displacement One of the most significant challenges of AI for the legal industry is the potential for job displacement. AI-powered tools can automate many tasks that were previously performed by human lawyers, such as document review and legal research. While this can increase

efficiency and productivity, it also raises concerns about the future role of lawyers in the legal industry.

2. Bias and Fairness AI systems are only as unbiased and fair as the data they are trained on. If AI systems are trained on biased data, they can perpetuate and amplify biases, leading to unfair outcomes. For example, AI-powered tools used in the criminal justice system may be trained on biased data, leading to discriminatory outcomes for certain groups. It is essential to ensure that AI systems are designed and trained with fairness and bias in mind.

3. Data Privacy and Security AI-powered tools rely on vast amounts of data to function, which raises concerns about data privacy and security. Lawyers and law firms must ensure that they are collecting and storing data in a secure and compliant manner. They must also be transparent about how they are using and sharing data with third parties.

4. Ethical and Professional Responsibilities AI is also raising new ethical and professional responsibilities for lawyers. Lawyers must ensure that they are using AI in a manner that is consistent with their ethical and professional obligations. For example, lawyers must ensure that they are maintaining client confidentiality and avoiding conflicts of interest when using AI-powered tools.

Conclusion AI has the potential to transform the legal industry, providing new opportunities for increased efficiency, improved decision making, and enhanced access to justice. However, it also presents significant challenges and requires careful consideration to ensure that it is used in a manner that is fair, unbiased, and consistent with ethical and professional responsibilities. The legal industry must embrace the opportunities presented by AI while also addressing the challenges it presents to ensure that it is used in a responsible and ethical manner. One of the key challenges is the potential for AI to perpetuate and even amplify existing biases, particularly in areas such as criminal justice where there are significant disparities in the treatment of different groups. Another challenge is the potential for AI to automate tasks traditionally performed by lawyers, raising questions about the role of legal professionals in the future and the need for new skills and training. Additionally, there are concerns around data privacy and security, as well as the potential for AI to replace human judgment and decision making entirely, leading to a loss of accountability and transparency. To address these challenges, the legal industry must engage in ongoing dialogue and collaboration with technology experts, regulators, and other stakeholders to develop ethical and effective frameworks for the use of AI in law. By embracing AI in a responsible and ethical manner, the legal industry has the potential to enhance its value and contribute to a more just and equitable society.

Conclusion
The Potential Future of AI in Law and Its Impact on Society

The development of artificial intelligence (AI) technology is rapidly transforming many industries, including the legal profession. The legal industry is now exploring various AI applications, such as contract analysis, legal research, e-discovery, and legal writing, to name a few. AI has the potential to revolutionize the way lawyers work, providing increased efficiency, improved decision making, and enhanced access to justice. However, the adoption of AI in law also presents significant challenges and raises ethical and professional concerns.

The potential benefits of AI in law are vast. One significant benefit is the potential to streamline legal processes, reducing the time and cost of legal work. For example, AI-powered contract analysis tools can quickly identify relevant clauses, extract data, and flag potential issues, saving lawyers hours of manual work. AI tools can also conduct legal research and analyze vast amounts of data in a fraction of the time it would take a human lawyer. This can lead to more informed decisions and better outcomes for clients.

Another benefit of AI in law is the potential to increase access to justice. AI-powered chatbots and virtual assistants can provide basic legal information and guidance to individuals who may not have access to a lawyer. This can help to bridge the justice gap and make legal services more affordable and accessible to all.

However, there are also significant challenges and ethical concerns associated with the adoption of AI in law. One of the most pressing concerns is the potential for AI to perpetuate and amplify biases. AI is only as good as the data it is trained on, and if the data is biased, then the AI will be biased as well. This can result in unfair outcomes and exacerbate existing inequalities in the justice system.

Another concern is the potential for AI to replace human lawyers. While AI tools can augment and enhance the work of lawyers, there is a risk that they could eventually replace them altogether, leading to job losses and reduced human oversight in the legal system. This could have significant implications for the justice system and the rule of law.

To ensure that the adoption of AI in law is responsible and ethical, the legal profession must address these challenges and concerns. Lawyers and legal professionals must work together with AI developers to ensure that AI is used in a manner that is transparent, accountable, and consistent with ethical and professional responsibilities. This will require ongoing dialogue and collaboration between legal professionals, AI developers, and policymakers.

In conclusion, the potential of AI in law is enormous, and its impact on the legal industry and society as a whole is significant. While there are challenges and ethical concerns associated with its adoption, the legal profession has an opportunity to embrace the benefits of AI while also ensuring that it is used in a manner that is fair, unbiased, and consistent with ethical and professional responsibilities. As such, the future of AI in law is one of collaboration, innovation, and responsible adoption.

The Importance of Continued Research and Development in AI for Law

The field of artificial intelligence has advanced significantly in recent years, and its impact on the legal industry is just beginning to be realized. The potential for AI in law is immense, and its use has already led to significant improvements in efficiency, decision making, and access to justice. However, the development of AI in law is still in its early stages, and continued research and development are necessary to fully realize its potential.

One of the key areas of research and development in AI for law is in the area of natural language processing. This technology has the potential to greatly improve the efficiency and accuracy of legal research, as well as the ability to analyze and interpret large volumes of legal documents. Additionally, advances in machine learning and predictive analytics can enhance the ability of lawyers to make informed decisions and provide more accurate and reliable legal advice.

Another important area of research and development in AI for law is in the development of algorithms and systems that are fair, unbiased, and consistent with ethical and professional responsibilities. As AI is increasingly used in decision-making processes within the legal system, it is important that these systems are transparent, accountable, and do not perpetuate existing biases and discrimination.

Furthermore, the development of AI for law also requires collaboration between legal professionals and AI experts. Lawyers and legal professionals must have a deep understanding of the legal system and the ethical implications of AI use, while AI experts must understand the intricacies of the legal profession and the specific needs of legal professionals.

In conclusion, the potential for AI in law is vast, and its impact on the legal industry and society as a whole is significant. Continued research and development in AI for law is essential to fully realize its potential, and it is important that this development is done in a manner that is fair, transparent, and consistent with ethical and professional responsibilities. By doing so, the legal industry can continue to leverage the benefits of AI while addressing the challenges it presents and ensuring that the use of AI in law benefits society as a whole.

The Need for Ethical and Responsible AI Development and Use in the Legal Industry

Artificial intelligence (AI) is transforming the legal industry, bringing new opportunities for increased efficiency, improved decision-making, and enhanced access to justice. However, as with any new technology, AI also presents significant ethical and legal challenges that must be addressed to ensure its use is fair, unbiased, and consistent with ethical and professional responsibilities. In this section, we will discuss the need for ethical and responsible AI development and use in the legal industry.

The Importance of Ethical and Responsible AI:

The rapid development and deployment of AI in the legal industry raise important questions about how the technology will be used and what impact it will have on society. The use of AI raises ethical and legal concerns, including issues related to bias, transparency, and accountability. These concerns are particularly relevant in the legal industry, where AI can have a significant impact on the lives of individuals, organizations, and society as a whole.

One of the most important ethical considerations when it comes to AI in law is the potential for bias. Bias can be introduced at many stages in the AI development and deployment process, including the data used to train the AI, the algorithms used to process the data, and the decisions made based on the output of the AI. Bias can have significant consequences, particularly in the legal industry, where decisions made based on AI output can have a profound impact on people's lives. To ensure that AI is used in a fair and unbiased manner, it is important to consider issues related to data quality, algorithmic transparency, and accountability.

Transparency and accountability are also essential when it comes to AI in the legal industry. It is important to ensure that AI systems are transparent and accountable, and that individuals and organizations have the ability to understand how decisions are made based on AI output. This requires that AI systems be designed in a way that allows for transparency and accountability, and that organizations be willing to provide information about how AI is used and the decisions made based on its output.

Another important ethical consideration is the need to ensure that AI is developed and used in a manner that is consistent with ethical and professional responsibilities. This requires that legal professionals and organizations be aware of the potential risks and benefits of AI, and that they take steps to ensure that the use of AI is consistent with ethical and professional responsibilities. This includes issues related to confidentiality, privacy, and the duty of care owed to clients.

Conclusion:

The development and deployment of AI in the legal industry has the potential to bring significant benefits, including increased efficiency, improved decision-making, and enhanced access to justice. However, it also presents significant ethical and legal challenges that must be addressed to ensure its use is fair, unbiased, and consistent with ethical and professional responsibilities. To address these challenges, it is essential that legal professionals and organizations embrace the need for ethical and responsible AI development and use, and that they take steps to ensure that the use of AI is consistent with ethical and professional responsibilities. Continued research and development in AI for law, with a focus on ethical and responsible AI development and use, will be essential in ensuring that AI is used in a manner that benefits society as a whole.

THE END

Key terms and definitions related to the topic of "AI Revolution in Law-Opportunities and Challenges" may include:

1. Artificial Intelligence (AI): A field of computer science and engineering that focuses on the development of intelligent machines that can perform tasks that typically require human cognition, such as learning, problem-solving, perception, and decision-making.

2. Machine Learning: A subset of AI that involves the use of algorithms and statistical models to enable computers to learn and improve from experience without being explicitly programmed.

3. Natural Language Processing (NLP): A branch of AI that focuses on enabling machines to understand, interpret, and generate human language.

4. Robotics: A field of engineering and science that deals with the design, construction, operation, and use of robots.

5. Big Data: Large and complex datasets that require advanced computing and analytics technologies to process and extract insights.

6. Intellectual Property (IP): Legal rights that protect the creations of the mind, such as inventions, literary and artistic works, symbols, and designs.

7. E-Discovery: The process of identifying, collecting, and producing electronically stored information (ESI) for use as evidence in legal proceedings.

8. Natural Language Generation (NLG): A form of AI that involves the use of algorithms to automatically generate human-like language and content.

9. Legal Writing: The process of creating legal documents, such as contracts, briefs, and memoranda, that communicate legal concepts and arguments in a clear and persuasive manner.

10. Ethics: The principles and values that govern human behavior and decision-making, particularly with respect to what is right and wrong. In the context of AI, ethics involves the consideration of issues such as bias, transparency, and accountability in the development and use of AI systems.

Potential References

Introduction:

- Floridi, L. (2019). Artificial intelligence, humanity, and the law. Philosophical Transactions of the Royal Society A: Mathematical, Physical and Engineering Sciences, 377(2144), 20180087.

Chapter 1: AI and Legal Research:

- Liu, Y., Pierce, B., & Sharma, D. (2019). Artificial intelligence and legal research. In Legal Informatics and E-Governance as Tools for the Knowledge Society (pp. 31-47). Springer.

Chapter 2: AI and Contract Review:

- Chakravarthy, G., Chaudhuri, S., & Narasimhan, S. (2019). Machine learning for contract review and analysis. In Artificial Intelligence and Law (pp. 165-180). Springer.

Chapter 3: AI and Predictive Analytics in Law:

- Katz, D. M., Bommarito, M. J., & Blackman, J. (2017). Predicting the behavior of the Supreme Court of the United States: A general approach. PLoS ONE, 12(4), e0174698.

Chapter 4: AI and Intellectual Property Law:

- Heinze, T., & Scepanovic, S. (2018). Algorithmic copyright enforcement in the EU—harmful or helpful?. Computer Law & Security Review, 34(5), 1119-1130.

Chapter 5: AI and E-Discovery:

- Da Silva, L. A., Gomes, R. M., & Carvalho, T. M. (2019). AI-assisted e-discovery: A systematic review. Computer Law & Security Review, 35(6), 105349.

Chapter 6: AI and Legal Writing:

- Voigt, B. (2019). Automated legal writing with artificial intelligence. In Legal Informatics and E-Governance as Tools for the Knowledge Society (pp. 49-63). Springer.

Chapter 7: AI and the Future of the Legal Industry:

- Kaminski, M. E. (2018). The right to explanation, explained. Harvard Journal of Law & Technology, 31(1), 1-54.

Conclusion:

- Schwartz, P. M. (2019). Artificial intelligence and the future of legal practice. Fordham Law Review, 88, 2595-2618.